Ankylosaurus

Written by Rupert Oliver
Illustrated by Bernard Long

© 1984 Rourke Enterprises, Inc.

Copyright © 1984 Martspress Ltd., Nork Way
Banstead, Surrey, SM7 1PB.

Library of Congress Cataloging in Publication Data

Oliver, Rupert.
  Ankylosaurus.

  Summary: Gentle Ankylosaurus has an eventful day
watching the meat-eating dinosaurs attack each other while she
forays for plants to eat.
  1. Ankylosaurus—Juuvenile literature.   [1. Ankylosaurus.
2. Dinosaurs]   I. Long, Bernard, ill.   II. Title.
QE862.065044   1984   567.9'7   84-17865
ISBN 0-86592-212-8

Rourke Enterprises, Inc.
Vero Beach, FL 32964

Rhamphorhynchus

Pteranodon

Pterodactyl

Ankylosaurus

Dimetrodon

Iguanodon

Tricondon

Ankylosaurus

Archaeopteryx

Ichthyosaurus

Plesiosaurus

Deinonychus

Nothosaurus

The sun was spreading its strong rays across the land. The mist of early morning had gone and a Stenonychosaurus had just returned from the hunt to rest. Its large eyes meant that it could hunt well in the dim light, catching animals that were still half asleep. However, the bright light of day hurt its eyes and Stenonychosaurus ran in to the bushes after a hard night's work.

The Stenonychosaurus had caught a small, furry mammal to eat. As it trotted toward the undergrowth with its prey, the Stenonychosaurus disturbed another dinosaur, the Ankylosaurus, who was bedded down nearby.

Ankylosaurus raised herself to her feet and smelt the air. It smelt clean and fresh. The weather had been growing warmer over the past few days. The insects buzzed in and out of the flowers. Soon it would be summer.

Ankylosaurus was hungry. She had to spend
nearly all the day eating to satisfy her hunger. There
were new shoots and young plants in the hills now.
The warmer days had brought them out.
Ankylosaurus liked to eat the new shoots. They were
juicy and tender. Some of the older leaves were too
tough to chew and during the winter Ankylosaurus
found very little food. Now that the warm weather
had come, there would be plenty of food.

Slowly, Ankylosaurus walked off in search of food. She soon came to a large bush covered in beautiful, sweet smelling flowers. Ankylosaurus was not interested in the flowers. She wanted to eat the tasty new leaves around the flowers.

As Ankylosaurus was happily munching away a Gravitholus ran past. Ankylosaurus did not often see bonehead dinosaurs such as this on their own. Perhaps the Gravitholus had lost a courtship fight.

As the sun climbed into the sky and the day became hotter, Ankylosaurus continued to eat. She chewed away happily on the young leaves of the bush. When she had finished these she moved on to the next bush. After a while, Ankylosaurus had eaten all the young shoots on the clump of bushes and she moved to look for more food.

Her search took her to the edge of one of the steep slopes that fell away to the lowlands. Below her, Ankylosaurus could see the thick vegetation that covered the land. A heat haze shimmered over the hot jungle. She saw another clump of bushes and turned to walk towards them.

As Ankylosaurus turned, a mighty roar filled the air and the ground rocked beneath her feet. In panic she looked around to see what could have caused such a frightening noise. Then it sounded even louder and the ground shook more violently. Ankylosaurus felt herself falling as the hillside collapsed beneath her. Her powerful legs could not hold on as she slipped down the steep slope.

No matter how Ankylosaurus struggled to find a foothold she just kept on slipping. She slipped and slid for a long time. When Ankylosaurus finally stopped, she was at the foot of a long, steep slope of gravel and loose soil. It was down this slope she had fallen.

Ankylosaurus was a little dazed, but she was not badly hurt. Her sudden arrival had started a Dromiceiomimus. The frightened dinosaur ran off into the bushes.

Ankylosaurus looked about her. Apart from the slope, she was surrounded by dense bushes and the air was hot and humid. There was no way she could climb back up the slope so Ankylosaurus pushed through the undergrowth.

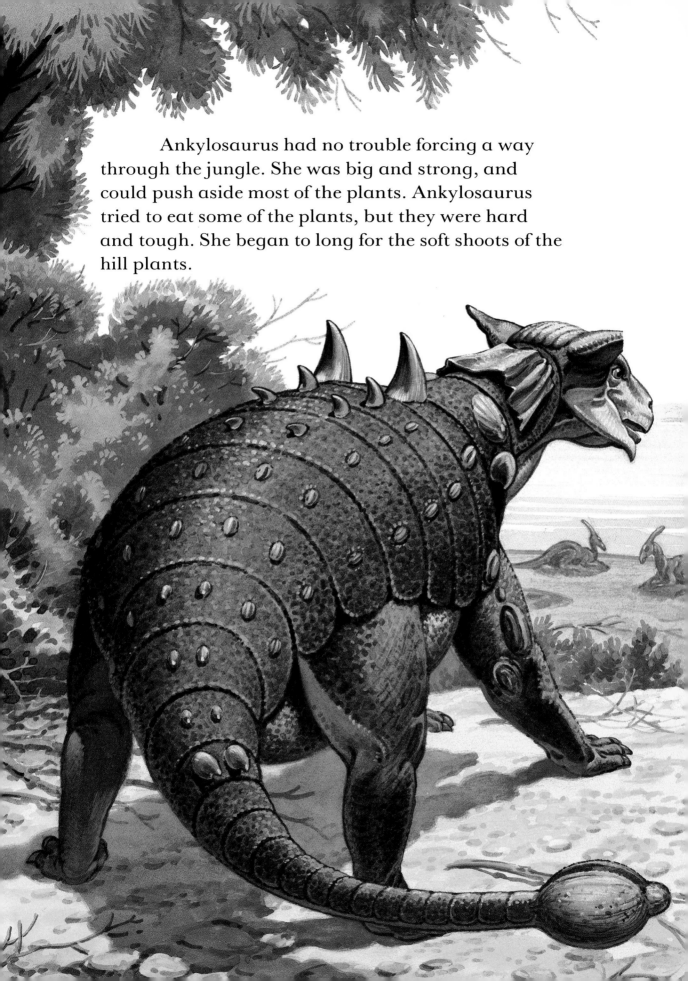

Ankylosaurus had no trouble forcing a way through the jungle. She was big and strong, and could push aside most of the plants. Ankylosaurus tried to eat some of the plants, but they were hard and tough. She began to long for the soft shoots of the hill plants.

Suddenly the jungle ended. Ankylosaurus
stood on a slight rise overlooking a river. Along
the sandy banks of the river were groups of
Parasaurolophus. Many of the duckbill dinosaurs
were crouched over mud nests that contained eggs.
As soon as they saw Ankylosaurus, a pair of large
Parasaurolophus ran toward her, uttering fierce
noises. Ankylosaurus was puzzled. Usually duckbills
were quiet and inoffensive. Now it looked as if they
would attack her. She decided to retreat into the
jungle.

As Ankylosaurus pushed her way through the undergrowth she realized it was getting less dense. Ankylosaurus also noticed that one of the plants had some tender new leaves on it. She stopped to eat.

There came a loud rustling noise from the depths of the jungle. A large animal was approaching Ankylosaurus. Ankylosaurus looked around to see what was coming and froze in sudden terror. The new charging animal was a ferocious Tyrannosaurus Rex. As Ankylosaurus watched in alarm another Tyrannosaurus appeared.

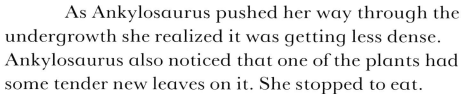

There was only one way that Ankylosaurus
would be safe from attack. She lay flat on the ground
and swung her clubbed tail around. The
Tyrannosaurus clawed savagely at Ankylosaurus
but her armor protected her. The tough bony shell
was strong enough to stop even the most powerful
kick from the hungry meat eater. For several
terrifying minutes the powerful killer dinosaur
clawed and bit at Ankylosaurus. At last
Ankylosaurus managed to hit one of the
Tyrannosaurs with her tail. The meat eater let out
a bellow of pain and rage. Then it moved away from
Ankylosaurus.

Suddenly another dinosaur appeared out of
the forest. The Alamosaurus had been feeding on the
tree tops but turned in alarm when she heard the
Tyrannosaurs. The Tyrannosaurs saw the
Alamosaurus. It would make a much easier meal
than Ankylosaurus, so they started to chase the
Alamosaurus.

Ankylosaurus remained flat on the ground. She was afraid the meat eaters would return. After a while Ankylosaurus stood up. She could not see the Tyrannosaurs. Perhaps they had caught the Alamosaurus and were busy eating. Ankylosaurus had been very frightened by the attack.

Ankylosaurus then decided to move on. The plants were more like those that she enjoyed eating. It seemed as if the ground was rising. Ankylosaurus was nearing her home in the hills. Then she heard the footsteps of a large animal behind her. She was alarmed in case it was another Tyrannosaur.

The newcomer was a Triceratops. The great horned dinosaur was a plant eater and would not attack Ankylosaurus. As she watched, the Triceratops started roaring and stamping the ground. Something was wrong.

Another Triceratops appeared. The two horned dinosaurs turned to face each other. Then they charged. The ground vibrated as the two heavy beasts approached each other. With a tremendous crash the dinosaurs met head on. They backed away from each other and charged again. The Triceratops were engaged in a courtship fight. Ankylosaurus watched them for a while, and then moved on in search of more juicy young shoots and leaves.

Ever since Ankylosaurus had left the river she had been traveling toward the hills. Now she found herself back among the bushes that she liked to eat.

As Ankylosaurus chewed hungrily on the tender shoots of the hill plants, the leaves suddenly parted. A small Parksosaurus shot out from cover. Hot on its heels came a Saurornitholestes. The chase continued until the Saurornitholestes leapt on the Parksosaurus and killed it. The vicious claw on the hind foot of Saurornitholestes brought down the other dinosaur with one blow.

Ankylosaurus took no notice of the chase. She was happy to be back among plants she could eat and where there was no sign of Tyrannosaurs. As the sun began to sink behind the horizon Ankylosaurus lay down and closed her eyes. It had been an eventful day and Ankylosaurus was very tired.

Ankylosaurus and Late Cretaceous North America

Length: 30 feet
Height: 9 feet

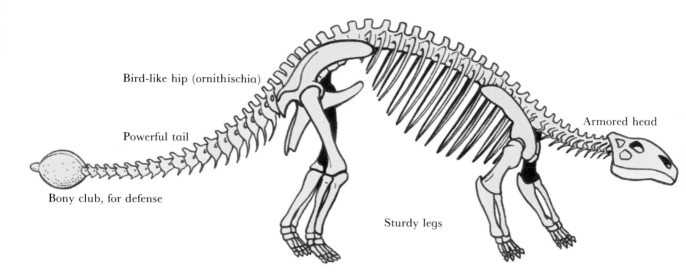

Bird-like hip (ornithischia)

Powerful tail

Armored head

Bony club, for defense

Sturdy legs

Skeleton of Ankylosaurus

When did Ankylosaurus live?

The Age of the Dinosaurs, or Mesozoic Era, began about 225 million years ago and lasted for some 160 million years. This immense length of time has been divided by scientists into three periods: the Triassic, the Jurassic and the Cretaceous. Ankylosaurus lived at the end of the third period, about 65 million years ago. It was one of the very last dinosaurs.

Where did Ankylosaurus live?

The fossils of Ankylosaurus have been found in the western part of North America, in the state of Montana and the province of Alberta. Today, this area of land is at the edge of the mighty Rocky Mountains which tower thousands of feet into the sky. When Ankylosaurus was alive, these mountains did not exist. In fact, the North American continent did not exist as we know it today. The earth movements that resulted in the formation of the Rockies, were, however, just beginning. The earthquake that flung Ankylosaurus down the slope in our story was a part of these earth movements. Across the millions of years, thousands of such earthquakes have pushed the rocks upwards to form the jagged peaks of today.

Today, to the east of the land where Ankylosaurus lived, are the Great Plains. 65 million years ago these did not exist either. A shallow sea stretched from the north of Canada through to the Gulf of Mexico. The world was a very different place when Ankylosaurus was alive.

The life of Ankylosaurus

Ankylosaurus belonged to one of the last and strangest groups of dinosaurs, the ankylosaurs. They first appeared during the early Cretaceous period, some 120 million years ago and lived a puzzling life. Ankylosaurus was around 30 feet long and weighed several tons, yet it had no teeth at all. Instead its jaws were covered in a horny beak. Scientists think that it probably ate soft plants and young shoots. Ankylosaur fossils are very rare. It is thought that this is because Ankylosaurus lived in the hills. The remains of animals that lived on high ground did not become fossilized easily. This may well explain the lack of Ankylosaurus fossils.

On its back the mighty Ankylosaurus carried a great weight of bony armor. Its tail ended in a heavy bone club that could have dealt a nasty blow to any attacker. Had a meat-eating dinosaur tried to attack Ankylosaurus, the plant-eater would probably have crouched down and swung its clubbed tail. It would have been impossible for any meat-eater to break through the armor and very difficult for it to overturn such prey. Even such a mighty hunter as Tyrannosaurus Rex would have found Ankylosaurus a very difficult animal to tackle.

Plants of the Cretaceous

At the time when Ankylosaurus lived, plants had been growing on dry land for nearly 300 million years, but in all that time there had not been a single flower. All the plants had been spore producers (gymnosperms). There were ferns, and horsetails and though there were conifers, there were no true flowering plants. In the mid-Cretaceous period all that was to change. For the first time in the history of the earth the plant life would have been recognizable to us today. There were many trees that we know well: oaks, willows, maples and even the fig tree. Among the smaller plants of the time were wild roses, grape vines and heather. Ankylosaurus must have encountered plants very similar to those of our time. It has been suggested that the toothless Ankylosaurus ate the soft fruits of the new flowering plants.

Cretaceous animals

It was not only the plants of the days of Ankylosaurus that would have been familiar to us. Many of the animals would have been, too. Insects had been around for many years and had become as familiar as the dragonflies and beetles on pages 10 and 11. Mammals had also been walking the earth for a long time. However, the most advanced mammal alive at the same time as Ankylosaurus was the small shrew-like creature that Stenonychosaurus has caught on page 5. Mammals such as lions, gazelle and elephants did not evolve for millions of years. Birds had first evolved during the Jurassic period, almost a hundred million years before Ankylosaurus. By the late Cretaceous they had evolved into several different types.

Of course, many animals alive during the Cretaceous were very different from today's creatures. The pterosaurs that flew in the air are now long extinct. The dinosaurs that were then so common have also died out and look very strange to our eyes.

Palaeoscincus, a relative of Ankylosaurus, had spikes to protect the sides of its body, but no bony club.